War-Wise and Other Poems

War-Wise and Other Poems

David J. Murray

iUniverse, Inc.
New York   Bloomington

Copyright © 2009 by David J. Murray

All rights reserved. No part of this book may be used or reproduced by any means, graphic, electronic, or mechanical, including photocopying, recording, taping or by any information storage retrieval system without the written permission of the publisher except in the case of brief quotations embodied in critical articles and reviews.

The views expressed in this work are solely those of the author and do not necessarily reflect the views of the publisher, and the publisher hereby disclaims any responsibility for them.

iUniverse books may be ordered through booksellers or by contacting:

iUniverse
1663 Liberty Drive
Bloomington, IN 47403
www.iuniverse.com
1-800-Authors (1-800-288-4677)

Because of the dynamic nature of the Internet, any Web addresses or links contained in this book may have changed since publication and may no longer be valid. The views expressed in this work are solely those of the author and do not necessarily reflect the views of the publisher, and the publisher hereby disclaims any responsibility for them.

ISBN: 978-1-4401-3473-9 (sc)
ISBN: 978-1-4401-3475-3 (dj)
ISBN: 978-1-4401-3474-6 (ebook)

Printed in the United States of America

iUniverse rev. date: 04/30/2009

Contents

Introduction i

War-Wise

A Child's Garden of Curses 1

A Searchlight's Day..2

A Thing of the Weasel Family...4

Time...5

Why?..6

Ghosts..7

Body Blow..8

Sparrows..9

Too Far Away..10

The Tandem and the Nightingale...................................11

Food...12

Fearmonger...14

For You..15

Trying Times...17

D-Day..18

Smiting...19

War...20

Two Girls 21

This Was My Burthen 22

Discussion Groups 23

Others 24

Requiescant 25

Cloudiness...26

Politics...28

Bonfire Night..29

Microcosms 31

Memoir #1 32

Memoir #2 34

Semi-Doggerel 35

Learning to Read 37

Wintersong 38

To Faust 39

To Falstaff 40

To Freud 41

Seagull 42

ONE HUNDRED MOOD STUDIES

Absence 45

Arc 46

Argent 47

Arms 48

Asphodels 49

Being 50

Birds 51

Blush 52

Burden 53

Clothes 54

Clouds 55

Dark 56

Darkness 57

Dawn 58

Dawns 59

Day 60

Doles 61

Dream #1 62

Dream #2 63

Dreamings 64

Dust 65

Earth 66

Eye #1 67

Eye #2 68

Eyes #1 69

Eyes #2 70

Eyes #3 71

Façade 72

Farewell 73

Feelings 74

Gains 75

Glances 76

Gloom 77

Gold 78

Hand 79

Impostor? 80

Jealousy 81

Knowledge 82

Land 83

Landscape 84

Light 85

Lines 86

Man 87

Marginality 88

Mind #1 89

Mind #2 90

Moment 91

Moments 92

Muse 93

Night #1 94

Night #2 95

Night #3 96

Night #4 97

Note 98

Nothing 99

Opportunity 100

Pain 101

Pearldom 102

Poems 103

Quietude 104

Rain 105

Rue 106

Sadness #1 107

Sadness #2 108

Sadness #3 109

Sadness #4 110

Sky 111

Sin 112

Smile #1 113

Smile #2 114

Snow #1 115

Snow #2 116

Strike 117

Summer 118

Sunlight 119

Sunshine 120

Temptation 121

Thought #1 122

Thought #2 123

Ugliness 124

Veil 125

Vein 126

Verse 127

Virtue 128

Warmth 129

Wastes 130

Winter #1 131

Winter #2 132

Winter #3 133

Wit 134

Wonderings 135

Wood 136

Words #1 137

Words #2 138

World #1 139

World #2 140

World #3 141

X 142

Y 143

Z 144

Introduction

The first set of poems in this volume is entitled War-Wise and was written in 2008. On September 1, 1939, when the war broke out, I had just turned two, and my father had moved the family from an inner-city region of Manchester, England, to what was then a "village" just beyond the green belt that surrounded the city's southern limits. Of course, nobody remembers much about what they experienced at the age of two; but the war was played out over the course of some six years, so that when the war in Europe ended on May 9, 1945, and the war with Japan ended on September 2, 1945, I was aged seven and eight respectively. This period was long enough for me to graduate from "infant school" (which I believe I entered at age four) to "primary school" (for children aged about six to eleven). I know I was attending the latter when the European war was in its final phases, because I am able now to recall, and write about here, several incidents that took place in that playground.

There are thirty-five poems in all, and they vary in form from free verse to rhymed stanzas. Some are "emotions recollected in tranquility," as Wordsworth phrased it, and some are musings about the war from an early twenty-first-century perspective. Some allusions might not be understood by readers who are neither British nor over retirement age, so I explain some of them here.

An "Anderson shelter" was a large hole dug into one's back garden and covered over with a corrugated metal roof, which itself was sometimes covered with earth and planted with grass. One entered the shelter by going down a step or two, and it was large enough to house a small family sitting or lying down on portable beds. The idea was that, when a pending air raid was announced by a very audible siren, the whole family would leave the house and spend the duration of the raid sheltered from, if not so much a direct hit by a bomb, at least the bricks and glass thrown about if a bomb scored a direct hit on one's house. People without Anderson shelters could either go to a communal brick shelter on a nearby street or stay in the house and take refuge under a table on the ground floor; few houses in Britain had cellars. A "blackout" was enforced as soon as night came on; heavy black curtains covered every window, and no lights were permitted to be visible from outside. We all learned that, apparently, a pilot several thousand feet up could see the light of a single match on the ground below.

Entertainment to keep everyone cheerful pervaded the radio waves whenever they were not actually broadcasting the news. Comedians who had once played the music halls found new careers in regular shows, and children were unwittingly exposed to an enormous array of popular songs (as well as to a surprising amount of classical music). One such song included the lyric "Daisy, Daisy ... on a bicycle built for two." That's the "tandem" in the title in one of the poems; the song had been written long before the war, in fact. Written during the war was "A Nightingale Sang in Berkeley Square," which is the nightingale alluded to in that same title. Also mentioned in that poem are two of the greatest lyric poets in German literature, namely, J. W. von Goethe (1749–1832) and H. Heine (1797–1856). Some of Heine's poems were set, unforgettably, to music by Robert Schumann (1810–1856).

References to English poetry in this set of poems are restricted to the work of W. Shakespeare (1564–1616). At the end of the set is a poem referring to Faust, the hero of Goethe's most ambitious play, who, tired of book-learning, conjured up Mephistopheles, who then introduced Faust to a variety of temptations; another poem refers to Sir John Falstaff, a nobleman-soldier who appears in several of Shakespeare's historical plays and who was notorious for his heavy drinking.

The second set I have called One Hundred Mood Studies. The word "study" is used here as it is in classical music: a short piece for piano that is deliberately designed for the improvement of a pianist's technique. Often studies are published in sets of one hundred or more. Certain composers, including M. Clementi (1752–1832) and C. Czerny (1791–1857), became famous for composing a steady stream of studies aimed at improving finger work, scale playing, and so on. But a few composers, including F. Chopin (1810–1849), F. Liszt (1811–1886), and A. Scriabin (1872–1915), wrote studies that were, yes, finger-breaking challenges, but also superb music in themselves, well worthy of inclusion in concerts and recitals. But whether you're playing a study by Czerny or a study by Chopin, the point is that you are exercising, practicing, honing your pianistic skills.

I deliberately chose to call this set of poems *studies* because, although each poem certainly has a meaning in its own right, each poem is also, from my point of view, an exercise in the crafts of word choosing, rhyming, and rhythm maintenance that have constituted the toolbox of the working poet for centuries. Most of the poems have meanings that are in the romantic tradition, wherein a poet wrote either to flatter the person to whom he or she was attracted or, alternatively, to let off steam about how disappointed he or she felt because of that person's apparent lack of interest in him or her. But these twin themes, in my experience, do not cluster and peak for a year or two when one is in one's twenties; they grip and buckle one's whole life from early adolescence onwards. Because so many poems concern the second of these themes, I thought of entitling the set One Hundred Studies in a Minor Key; at another time, I thought of the title Broodings and Moodinesses. But One Hundred Mood Studies won out as my final choice of title for this set. Please note that the title of each poem is drawn from the first line of that poem. In most cases, but not all, the title also describes the contents of the poem as a whole.

As with my earlier volumes, *Confusion Matrix and Other Poems* and *Surface Tension and Other Poems*, I am extremely grateful for the exceptionally competent editorial and design teams of iUniverse Inc. for their help in preparing this work for publication. And, of course, my gratitude to Sylvia Hains, Christine Hains, Esther Murray, and Rachel Breau is as deep as ever. I am especially indebted to Barbara and Kenneth Norwich for suggesting that I write the set I entitled War-Wise.

War-Wise

A Child's Garden of Curses

When I was maybe eight or so,
With childhood friends I used to go
To a private place in a private glade
At the end of a garden that none of us knew;
Here, like pirates, we sat in its shade
Admiring the secret den we had made.

That we stole apples, I cannot disclaim;
But I also remember finding a name
To remember it by, after its loss;
For the very next day, from its shrubberied edge,
Its owners appeared. They dragged us across
Their nettles and over their lawn to their house

And through French windows into their study
With carpet and desk; bedraggled, unsteady,
We stood in a row while the wife took the phone,
All ready to notify police of our crime;
The husband had asked her to call, but his tone,
When he spotted how frightened we all had grown,

Was audibly softened; no phone call was made;
Out we were ushered, and thus lost our glade.
But I knew I'd remember it, due to its name:
I had called it "Green Patch" in a moment of joy.
But violence had ruined our pirate-like game;
Once you've been frightened, you're never the same.

For I have to report now that, quite undesigned,
A memory suddenly came to my mind
As I actually wrote the above on our fears;
Before he had dragged us, the husband had hit us,
And headed for me—but, on seeing my tears,
Had stopped short; I'd repressed this for years.

A Searchlight's Day

My wartime blitz—oh, such impoverished arms
They seemed, the streaks of the lines of the searchlights' rays
Probing, like lasers, the uninvited clouds,
Dabbling, like pretenders, with benighted powers,
Moving, keeping their limbed antennae straight
Like the Twentieth Century Fox studio's beams,
Aimed to enhance the legends of their stars,
Up to where renegade stars, from real constellations,
Also shone bleakly, down through the clouds, on Manchester.

Those searchlights, so like toys, so fragile, moved
Like little machines by unmachine-like men,
Yearned to cause an engine's roar to sputter,
Yearned for a flickering flame from a fuselage;
Hungry tongues of illuminated air they were,
Hungry arms of untroubled warfare-lust
That reached *ad astra* for an unheard grunt,
And a falling spiral of unfrantic fire
That dived right down, past a grille of pencil'd lights,
To the black silence of an unexpecting Earth.

The lights moved on, around, roaming the sky,
And found the bailed-out pilot on his way down,
Down along the arc-light of a beam
That held him in place, a captured moth,
While ambulances and police cars poked the night
With their on-the-way-to-help impacting noises
(No lights allowed) to where they thought
The pilot would touch down; down he came, grim,
Ashen, angry at being taken prisoner;

His parachute was disentangled; then alone
He stood in a field, then was escorted, walking
Staunchly through the dark and drip-wet fields
To streets where waited the vehicles he expected;
A small crowd waited there, curious to see
The enemy; some women brought him cups of tea;
Some men gave him cigarettes—"Poor soul, he must
Be cold"—the searchlights stanched their lights and vanished.

A Thing of the Weasel Family

A thing of the weasel family is
The fisher; it eats coldly, unviciously,
But killingly; like many predators,
It goes for the underjaw of its prey
To bring it down and silence it;
Normally, it will not eat the head
Of its victim, just the hindquarters.

When Nature breeds War, fishers among men
Sign up for killing, but—
Unlike the fishers among the animals—
They are cruel, hotly, viciously,
Vivaciously; War spreads contagion
Of soul-death through its practisers;
Animals seem saints alongside men.

Time

The clocks are tired of telling Time
That Time can never stop;
No matter what the daytime brings,
The seconds tick like living things
And, all night long, Time keep.

Time seems incessant when the sky
Delivers intermittent doom;
Each waiting minute lasts for hours;
The sky fills up with clouds and showers;
And then the bombing starts again—

Sometimes the blast sounds far away—
Somebody else is crouched beneath
His table, while the heavens roar
As if they'd been in Hell before
And relished dropping death;

Time cannot tell when Time has stopped,
But you have a soul, and it can feel;
And when *your* tabletop starts to shake,
And your walls to creak, and your roof to break,
Nothing but Time seems real.

Why?

Could I cognize what mystic layers deep
Structure the world's incongruence, making sense
Of what is so incursive to one's heart
That sense is a thing too present, as sensation,
To be interpreted in reasoned terms,
Then perhaps Philosopher I'd be;
But not right now, for no philosopher
Can know the right from wrong, just given truth;
Philosophers cannot speak on truth until
Their minds have caved in to the majesty
Of biological law; between the becks
Of ravenous needs and reproductive yens,
They waver, bovine with a human bent
For rumination on their beds of facts.

Ghosts

In Sunday school, we sometimes drew
Pictures whose innocence shone through
The spattered lines of gunshot fire
That dotted and dashed each page entire
Until, on the page, a Messerschmidt
Was finally and firmly hit
And fell in flames into the blue
Of our crayon'd sea; we drew no crew.

These, the machines, were in crayon drawn;
Our tracer bullets skirted the dawn,
Or courted the night with targeted flare
Winging across the paper's air;
We'd scrawl a whirl of crayon'd black
Accompanied by an "Ack-ack-ack!"
We'd scatter a Wedgwood of golden flames
Onto our pictures that had no names.

A postwar film, well worth the viewing,
Shows General Patton silently seeing
An African carnage through Carthage's eyes,
While ghostly music glosses the skies.
Our Sunday school classroom was warrior-free;
No Romans or Spartans stood by me;
But ghosts of their children still knowingly stare
At our sad little sketches of death in the air.

Body Blow

The bonds that hold us fettered in our place
Are limn'd from Providence, not Grace;
Pure chemistry, atomic spheres, though light,
Score their incredible scores, yet never quite

Relieve us of our freedom to feel free;
We cannot see the woodlands for the sea;
Our biochemical calls are urgent ones;
They separate the moonlight from strong suns;

And, as the path we tread grows ever steeper,
We laugh at the silliness of a "Grim Reaper";
Death has no personage or *caractère*;
It is an abstract noun of thinnest air;

Yet the fetters remain. We know our slotted place;
And, when we seek to flee from sheer disgrace,
We wander, we bump into unripe apple trees,
So shuttered are our guilty memories.

I heard, more than once, in England's green
And pleasant land, epithets obscene
From children and from house painters, applied
To persons not indigenous, born outside;

By Providence, these persons were endowed
With ties that seemed unseemly to the crowd;
So, close around us lurked, largely unseen,
A venom of whose power I'd never been

Aware before; its basic wrongness routed
An optimism I had never doubted,
Until those simple epithets hurt my ears,
And lanced what little joy had laced my tears.

Sparrows

I cannot calculate what mighty weights
Went into your thinking when you questioned me
And asked me to show my childhood in a war
So reprehensible in origin
That sparrows on a wall, unable to phrase
Our hatreds for us, run to snatch up crumbs
Scattered by a lady on some grass
Sprawling along the bottom of their wall;
And Prose, that endless pedlar of the Real,
Looks splitted and chopped like this, with not a hope
Of spinning a weave of Hope within its words;
It droops into shock when it sees how prejudice
Does nothing to stop our sparrows from thinking of nothing.

Too Far Away

My war is far too far away for grief
To have spread its dreadful colours through my mind;
I had no time of unremitting pain
To plant as scaffold for my history;
Nor did I lose my raptor'd fellow-friends
Or see my parents crumpled on the ground;
I have no right, because I have no grief,
To capture what I know in dirgic sound;
I am a hypocrite compared with you
Who read these words and paw away the air
Between us, hurling off my nuisance self,
Leaving more space for those whose *raisons d'être*
Are to usurp the souls of those who can't
Restore the souls of those already dead.

The Tandem and the Nightingale

Beyond the tandem and the nightingale
Hailed in the songs we sang in World War II
Stood the dark *Lieder* of the Fatherland,
Songs that few Allied soldiers sang or knew.

One could hear, in the cresting tramp of Nazidom,
Brutalizations of poetry's designs;
The poetry of Heine, set by Schumann,
Were not the common words of Fritz or Hans;

But backwards it also worked, the other way;
I was walking to school on a greyish September morn
When a Polish workman of strapping middle age
Put down his spade and, in a voice that held no scorn,

Quoted, at the sight of me, some words
That Shakespeare had embedded in a tale:
"And then the whining schoolboy, with his satchel
And shining morning face, creeping like snail

Unwillingly to school." I dared not move;
I had heard greatness talked by a foreign tongue;
And he, looking askance at my bewilderment,
Wondered aloud that I should be so young

As not to know who wrote those sceptr'd lines.
Back to his work he turned, but I felt worse,
For I had learned that a learned foreigner,
Accent and all, could freeze my mind with verse.

Food

It was so fixed, that paltry regimen,
That what I liked to eat stood firmly out:
Anything minced meat, potato-ey,
Anything bread-ey or corned-beef-ey,
Bramble seedless jam, drippings on toast,
And treat of treats, butter-and-sugar balls,
And sausages, and trifle (rare!), and sweets,
And chip butties, and fried bread, and scrambled egg.

After the war came the first banana,
The first ketchup, the first ice cream;
Canada first swam into my mind
When, at school, we were given tins
Of drinking chocolate, a gift from a land
Known to me only by a novel,
Ungava by R. M. Ballantyne,
With man-killing bears stalking the snows.

Getting that chocolate home was war itself;
Round each corner lurked the threat of "Kids!"
(Our nomenclature for the larger boys)
Who hoped to steal our stuff and run away;
Older or the same as us,
Perpetual threats; our matinees
On Saturdays at the cinema revealed
Movies with outlaws who behaved like those "kids."
Warfare was there at home, 'twixt "kids" 'n me—

Except of course for my little friends
With whom I would run off searching
O'er frost-drawn fields and under skies
Cloaked with a grey unknown elsewhere
(So dark that once, in a schoolroom book,
I saw a sky with a colour false
And complained the book was "Wrong, miss, 'cos
No sky is ever blue!"); searching,

I said, for something, I'm still uncertain what,
And got into trouble at home for running off
To see my Grandma two hundred miles away,
Or to take my imagined offspring by the hand,
For a walk, or to savour distant mental vistas,
And, strange to say, unknowingly, as I walked,
I never stopped to bother about food.

Fearmonger

The hollow hawk of death denies
What human light shines in his eyes;
He tries to be a horrid skull
Until he feels his eyes fill full
Of tears and tries, in vain, to pull
Them back and once more terrorize

The shifty souls who stare at him
As if he were a Gorgon grim,
Ready to freeze, into their place,
Those idiots who tried to face
Him, but themselves disgrace
When they fall back into whimperdom.

But now he is tired of holding court
To a hollow throng in a war too short;
Should he not put his gaze away
And store it aside for a rainy day
And, in the meantime, see that play
Where a king breaks a jester's heart for sport?

For You

And we will cross, will you and I,
All barriers of time;
A child were you and a child was I,
Unknown to us was crime;

We knew of tantrums and of laughs,
We knew of loss and fear,
But neither knew of the photographs
That soon were to appear;

We knew of food and of exotic fun,
And the wildest West was ours;
The cinema told of Bad undone
And of Virtue's sweetest powers.

It told of dogs that were loved beyond
A simple desire to please;
It told of a Mickey Mouse too fond
Of his Pluto, his Minnie, his cheese.

And the cinema told us of high romance
Striding across the seas,
While the music surged in an endless dance
Round Technicolor trees.

Neither knew yet of the flickering glare
Of those documentaries
That showed the prison camps as they were,
Living cemeteries;

We did not know that, here to stay,
Were films that showed all kinds
Of things that would never go away
From our tender-hearted minds;

They shattered Mickey Mouse to muck;
Eyeglasses stared *en masse*
At the camera's eye as it slowly took
Their pictures on each pass;

A mental line shows where I lost
My childhood's innocence;
The impact of the Holocaust
Would wipe out all my sense

That the world was good and filled with love.
I'd spend my later years
Scanning the world as if to prove
The rightness of my fears—

That I, like you, could a victim be
Of the crass and the gross, who hate
All serious soliloquy,
Then unite to desecrate

The sublime, the inspired, the ideal.
A lamppost stood outside
My house; I dreamed that there, for real,
A gathering soldiery vied

To hang me from that lamppost's height;
I wakened from that dream,
But still I think, when I think of that night,
Of my barely choked scream.

Trying Times

War traps, in its tenacious jaw, all hope
That laughter or, in turn, a listlessness
Would sweep the household from its daily wheels
Of duties and committees, smiles and frowns;
War bites hope down, gulping it into a maw
Already full of sufferings and limbs
And spectacled mountains—oh, those photographs!

War is no goddess, but a male tenacious,
Whose loin-girt madness praises others' pain,
And hurls the witness of its own heroics
(Witness unwritten because those heroes died)
Into a pit of thoughts and yet more thoughts
And more thoughts still, all of these unliving;
What is a thought can never live, just rot
In a sandhill box that calls wars "games."

Men make of aggression something virtuous
And make, of vice, reward for the aftermath
Of watching oneself re-kill; war adds
A spicy sperm of venom to the fact
That the "meaning of life" is a term devoid of meaning;
For things that are living are there, uncorrupt,
And only the things that the living have thought,
Or spoken, or moulded into an artifact,
Can be said to have meanings; war is a strategy
For spreading spoilsport over all domestic;
Zeus pins Athena to the barroom floor.

D-Day

The enemy's bombs dropped hard upon the beach;
To the dying man, grasping at dawn, appeared
The dawn, but jocund Day lay out of reach,
And Night loomed closer than he'd ever feared.

Smiting

Outside, the night is black and also deathly still;
There are animals around, poised to pounce and kill,
While I am writing these lines somewhat against my will.

And in the pitch-black womb of warring's worldly Night,
Humans were there, poised to smash and spoil and smite,
And for me to write against them is maybe not quite right;

So into a night must *I* escape, a locality where
Razors meet landscapes and rivers smooth the ribald air;
There it is peaceful, because there's nothing really there.

War

When that Destruction, with its groping hand,
Reaches to filch the surface from the world
And scars a city's streets to disemboweled,
And razes fields to sodden empty land—

And when that you hear a choir's rich harmony
As it raises its uplift song of battles won
Until a stirring entry of diapason
Bids it be seated to hear a homily

Dedicated to the praise of war—
Then you feel free to cast your mind around
From palace walls to trodden clifftop ground
And on and on to distant places far;

War has breathed Future on this stony Earth;
War is a child who questions not his birth.

Two Girls

O you two girls who walked down Princess Street
On a sunny day of September two-oh-eight,
I was behind you, staring, captivate
At the golden fall of the blonden hair, yellow,
Of you on the left, and the cropped and jetted black
Of you on the right, both of you strong and sweet,
But far beyond desiring of the fellow
Each of you knew was staring at your back.

Oh, what a blaze of glory it could be
To lie with you both, blond and black alone
In a bed that knew nothing of hearth or heath or home,
Just an encounter with colour and smooth limbs
To pour into a poem lasting all day long
Creating myths in verses that would see
Fanciful conquests born from idle whims,
Wistful thinking burgeoning into song!

But why on earth is all this footling rhyme
Here, in a volume remembering the war
As a dreadful thing emerging from before,
When I was too child to feel an adult's pang?
Had they been born in nineteen-twenty-five,
Blond and jetted black, transported where
My street had a lamppost where later I might hang,
Maybe they'd also hang, because unfit degenerates.

This Was My Burthen

This was my burthen, my tether-tree, my yoke:
Two women had I: a mother who knew well
How to enclothe and feed me, and could spell
Words like "café" that seemed to me a joke,
And could count on our bright and carefree Christmases
To prove to us the Lord had *us* for witnesses;

And neighbour had I, whose house was full of books;
She often played her Beethoven sonata;
She had an etching of a scene from Goethe;
She filled a bookcase with volumes thick whose looks
Were heavy, glossy, sturdy; some monographs
Held painted landscapes that vied with lithographs.

Two women had I: the one who made me take
My daily bread before I left for school
And taught me life's morals and the golden rule,
To give to others only what I'd like
To have from them; and the one whose heart
Shared with me manna crystallized as art.

Discussion Groups

And now the blood comes thick and furious fast
Into my brain; I see august conclaves
Of worthy bishops, trappingly bedecked,
Pondering, brooding, wondering if a war
Could ever "worthy" be, and then agreeing
That, provided it were fought in self-defense,
A war could be a conduit for a freeing.

But there are others whose blood is thick and fast
And eager to spite; they gather up in waves,
Warriors buckled in unfeigned disrespect,
Shieldings held in readiness before
Bodies bulked with armour, bold, expressing
Impatience for an opening offense,
In a war whose only purpose is aggressing.

And when the time for battle comes at last,
And the ranks of bullies, patriots, and knaves,
Gathered in blossoming phalanxes, expect
Spears to be hoisted and swords to be thick with gore;
Then will the skies seem unpleasant, and, fleeing,
The victims will pray to be rescued, and, immense,
The skies will say nothing, silent, unspeaking, unseeing.

Others

Are others' eyes as beautiful as yours?
Some come close; some are clearly not;
But what is mystery is how their cloistered light
Adds to, or subtracts from, what we've got,
A slow and glistering longing that survives
No matter who the partners in our lives.

The long glistering lingers from the war;
I saw its hinted beauties from the time
I stupidly waived submission to a girl,
The first, she would have been; this crime
Of soulmate gaming I regret;
Perhaps atonement can I hope for yet.

But fear from that war stalked my every pace;
And poison puked, like Destiny, in my face.

Requiescant

They seemed a promising start-point for a verse,
These lines that formed full-fledgèd in my mind:
"Murderous was the veil that hovered low
Over the walls of a Europe long ago"—
But World War II was never long ago,
Nor ever will be, for, when dead and gone
Are those who lived it but survived, the dead
From the war, whose bodies caked the fields
Or, frozen, lay prone on a frozen prison ground,
Or, buried, lay broken beneath a house of bricks,
Will never have names just jotted into lists;
Their names will live on the walls of schools and churches,
And, even though those walls may suffocate
Beneath the onslaughts of unfaith, those names,
The dead of World War II, will soldier on.

Cloudiness

I praised the skies once, grey up high and piled;
Hardly a blue showed in that Northern sky;
It lay above all deeds and thoroughfares,
And, if I thought it grand, I was a child
Who had seen nothing of blueness undefiled
And had no need its cloudiness to decry.

Silver and sleek shone the cobbled streets
That told of rain just recently gone by;
The rain was incessant prelude to dull weeks
When, at Saturday matinees, we'd dispel
The gloom with a Western and a serial
About a spaceship or about a spy,

Those lovely mornings when we had no school;
But, on the Monday next, we'd troop to play
In the playground, where we'd ask and ask and ask
The janitor to tell us when the war would end,
And he would guess, "Tomorrow," and then send
Us off, while he resumed his working day.

None of us knew why it would be so good
That the war should end, except that we would live
More easily and peacefully; so we would ply
The janitor with "When will it end?" while there
He stood and smiled, breathing the morning air;
"Today" was an answer he would never give

Because, one morning, the radio told us all,
That the war in Europe had indeed been ended.
We all cheered when the janitor confirmed for us
That the news was correct; we continued to play,
Not knowing we'd commemorate that day
For the rest of our living years; but, unintended,

A consequence silently waited for us from this
That would spoil our schoolboy Saturdays forever
And turn our classrooms into scholars' dens;
While we'd been hounding the janitor for news,
Out in the battle, teams of newsreel crews
Had filmed, over the sea, the end-of-war endeavour

That had crossed the European plains to where
Attractive hills, like a theatre's summer set,
Greeted the dawns with splendorous affray
And sank, at nightfall, into a soothing black;
Nobody knew that, behind them, at the back,
Were prison camps nobody would forget.

Nothing can mask, from my memory's mind, the sound
Of collective shock, a spasm of grown-up sigh,
When we saw the newsreels from those hidden places;
A man, skeletal, was praying (for death?) as he lay
On a stretcher some soldiers were carrying away;
This photo will blight my life until I die.

Politics

Political poems exist, but they are fraught
With baggage uninspired; they're crass with thought;
Little there is that's worthy to be taught;
And much of what there is, is what there's not:

Communes, wherein no greed is thought to be;
Tyrannies, whose servant-soldiery
Readily taxes a saddened peasantry
To raise high monuments unto eternity;

Theocracies, whose priests have private lines
To gods who, of human mercy, show few signs;
Warlorded worlds, whose rulers have designs
To scatter private thoughts with guns and mines;

And, even in democracy's fresher air
Competitors fierce can clamour that it's fair
To pass discriminative laws to scare
People away for whom they do not care—

Oh, how boring it is to sit and this to pen!
All that I want is peace to read and write
And make, in my work, a place of naked Night,
Where bullies must lose, and music win again.

Bonfire Night

During the war, a celebration held
Every November in Britain had to be cancelled:
Bonfires and fireworks were involved at night;
But at night a state of blackout was enforced
Across the clouded country just in case
An enemy bomber saw a light below
And from it inferred the presence of a town.

In fact, my father's evening job consisted
Of helping when an air-raid headed over;
He helped with disrupted lives and buildings downed
Immediately in the aftermath of a raid
And didn't say much about the things he saw.

But every night's beginning saw a ritual:
First, draw the blackout curtains tight
Ensuring that no light could shine through chinks;
When curtain-pulls imperfect were, a knock
At the door meant reprimand from a warden
Whose job it was to tramp through every street
Checking that all was all as dark as possible.

Second, we children went to bed, but lay
Fixed in a darkness where all sounds seemed louder,
Especially footsteps in the street; we learned
That female footsteps went a-clackety-clack,
Faster than a man's deliberateness.
But then, not every night, but many a night,
The wailing of the air-raid siren washed

Its warning across the darkness and the night;
Up we'd all get, dressing gowns on, or, if
A child were sleeping, he'd be carried in
The arms of a parent into the night and down
A few steps into the Anderson shelter.

Sometimes we saw the night sky lit aloft
With roaming searchlights moving to and fro;
Sometimes we heard loud bangs, saw sudden flashes;
Perhaps an anti-aircraft gun's ack-ack
Divided the night into more than flash and thump—
These we could hear as we sat inside the shelter,
Perched on bunks. We sometimes got a treat
Or something hot like a drink or tasty snack
That made the shelter like a Boy Scout camp
With midnight feasts in tents in thunderstorms.
My father, meanwhile, would have left and gone
To where he was sent, wherever bombs had hit;
We never knew, or asked, to where he'd been.

After the raid, an "all clear" sound, continuous,
Filled up the night again, and so to bed
Went sleepy-headed we and back to sleep;
But for six years, all that we knew of fireworks
Came from those glimpses of those warring skies
With searchlights' ambient rays scanning across
The inevitable underclouds of night,
Where rarely a star emerged to try to shine.

After the war, we learned to re-light fires
And set off fireworks in our own back gardens
To celebrate the death of one Guy Fawkes,
A seventeenth-century traitor who had tried
To blow up the seat of government in England;
He died in a death so awful for his crime
That Britain and brutishness still in my mind concur.

Microcosms

Small microcosms of the world
Were British schools back then:
Boys and girls separate,
The playground divided by a wall
So low that, during playtime, when
The girls would stand upon their hands
By the schoolhouse building, unseen bands
Of boys could watch their skirts down-fall
Giving each leaden boy a fix
Till playtime came around again;
And the winds blew wild in the tousled hair
Of the girls whose legginess lit the air,
Shamelessly showing they didn't care;

And games were for boys who didn't care
If fun changed to bullying now and then;
Thugs and victims, both innate,
Tempted each other to recall
The logical legerdemain
Where every victim understands
That the bully schemes seditious tricks
To lure the victim to where he stands
And machinates the victim's fall
To the ground by fisticuffs, wrestles, and kicks
Until the victim weeps again
And the bully stops, with a gracious air,
As if he were always playing fair
And the world were on his side for ever.

Memoir #1

We thought that war was normal,
A nuisance, but not to disdain;
In our Sunday schools and classes
We prayed to God to win
And forgot to ask if the Deity
Knew aught of German piety.

So childish were our thoughts of war
That a sputt'ring plane going down the sky
In a plume of black and a flare of flame
Was just an enemy going to die;
We assumed that our Heaven's cherubim
Would never say a prayer for him.

So idiotic were we then
That the bombs that bombed us every day
Could only take another's life
And never take our own away;
But, if it did, *as* children, we
Were sure of a place at our Good Lord's knee.

So, with composure, I learned to read
And to write my name at an age so rare
That my teachers moved me up a year,
To a school with older youngsters there;
I was brought and displayed to an older class
As a child so bright that I could pass

For one of them in my classroom skills;
But I was shaking in my boots,
For there, at a desk in the very front row,
Was a girl who had laughed when some older brutes,
Who had caught me in a local park,
Had dragged me into a shelter's dark,

Where a pile of dog poop, stinking, lay,
And forced my head down to sniff at it
While this girl, with others, laughed away
As, wriggling, I smelled that shit;
I asked in that classroom what I had done
To be moved to a class where this girl was one

Of my classmates; I dared, as I stood, afraid,
There at the front of her class, to set
My eyes on her face to figure her mind;
Would she laugh at me more? Would she mock when we
    met?
But her face returned blankness, and I knew then
She would leave me alone and not hurt me again.

Memoir #2

There was also a boy, I regret to say,
Who really enjoyed taking joy away
From others who would friendly be;
If they moved close, he'd push them aside
In deliberate effort to hurt their pride,
And, for some reason, he'd picked on me.

We were a group then, three or four,
Who swapped our treasures and proudly bore
Our comic books to each other's places
And, out of Meccano, constructed cranes
Or wobbly cars or decrepit trains,
Putting ourselves through an engineer's paces,

Until one day, one afternoon,
I proudly displayed a thing I'd done
From Meccano, constructed with nut and bolt;
I turned my back, and, fast as light,
He tried to unloosen each nut that was tight,
And to ruin my work and to dub me a dolt.

And, suddenly, something rose up, a black,
An anger I had been holding back,
And I jumped at his head, with both of my fists
Flying around his cheeks and his ears,
And I beat him down till I heard his tears,
But I did not stop, and my tiny wrists

Continued to maelstrom about his head;
I did not care if I punched him dead—
At least it was me who was sitting atop
His howling mess—they dragged me away,
My mother and his; but, on that day,
I learned that a bully, if bullied, will stop.

Semi-Doggerel

Kittens have claws, but also need
A furry love; their hearts can bleed
Like ours, but not for the things we want;
Our wants are multiple, theirs are scant:
We want respect, which comes from power
And money; kittens want an hour
Of stroked purring, a litter-box clean,
And sofas and posts to scratch upon.

Kittens never manufacture fame
From a lifetime spent ensuring that their name
Not figure in a one-day news obit
That death has come, and that's the end of it;
Nor have they stomach for attacks by groups
That muster, with rewards, a gang of troops
To spread despair among communities
That have no everyday amenities.

Kittens will never morph the Universe
Into a Cat who lets the vast discourse
Of mathematics idle to a halt
While kittenish minds across its beauties vault,
Assigning to a star a fate, or to a rock
A destiny, and every brain-work mock.
Kittens are free to be what they can be;
Only humans are law-locked, trapped in enmity.

Art cannot free humans, nor can Song;
Only obedience carries them along,
While all a kitten needs are cute, sharp claws;
Its scratching-post is not a Primal Cause
Created by Cat; the post was made by Man
Who, trying to be as Animal as he can,
Can often fail, and fall to such a mood
That anger and fear become betrothed to blood.

So all a man can do is fight,
With a minstrelsy born of fear and fright,
In a war that he hopes will bring him fame
Or even a monument keeping his name
Alive and deathless in churches and schools
Until, perhaps, a potentate rules
That wars should be stopped, perhaps by force,
And Natural Law re-shape its course.

Learning to Read

Give me a farm-death, neat and quick;
Animal corpses, white and black
Strung out to hang upon a rack,
Were born to eat and breed and die—
And so was I;

Please take away those corpses shot,
Still dressed in their snowy hats and coats,
Still wearing their broken working-boots,
Their flesh as white as the snowy ground
Where they lie;

When I saw those photos in that book,
I curled with anguish, for, where had stood
Eyes, were holes of blackened blood;
I had assumed those eyes gouged out,
But maybe not;

For crows of the field may, ravenous, have come
To peck at the two things they could eat
That were not too hard, but as rich as meat,
On those frozen corpses, stiff in a row,
In the snow;

And what their names were, I know not;
The book was written as foreigners write;
But my face must have shown my soul's affright,
For the person who chanced on me reading that book
Was horror-struck.

Wintersong

Do I detect brown leaves upon the lawns?
Winter has blown us its first initial breath,
And the colours will go, and, leafless, the branches feign death
And a pink in the East will forecast Winter's dawns.

When I was a child, the winters were much less cold;
The schools were busy and all the classrooms full,
The newsreels ensured that our lives were never dull,
And our bodies grew as we watched the war unfold;

And in those winters, music sang like Spring;
A clatter of Clementi I recall
From the neighbour's piano, and the Music Hall
On the radio had songs on everything;

A deepened mood had graced the Universe;
Whoever heard a violin soar in a snatch
Of splendour, or a piano run to catch
A rainbow in a prelude, knew that worse,

Much worse, would be the sounds of war;
So we would hunker down, in Britain's grey,
Hoping to hear great music every day,
And never muffled gunfire from afar.

To Faust

Over every mountaintop is peace.
Treetops betray to you but little breeze;
The little birds are silent in the trees;
Soon, soon, you too will find release—

For, thanks to your meddlings in art,
And palimpsestic dabblings in science,
And fiddlings with a futile necromance,
You were a scholar who had lost his heart;

You'd had it with your philosophic charms
And wanted to throw out your volumes' rows;
You'd had enough of dithyrambic prose
And of statues that felt hollow in your arms;

But from all of this, one day, you will be free.
Age will make all these pestilences go;
Reading becomes too hard, writing too slow;
Then you will rest, but only peaceably

When a question you ask attains a resolution;
This question will stain your golden mountaintops,
And trees will tremble, until your questioning stops:
How can you, from your shame, find absolution?

To Falstaff

Are you, Falstaff, sickened by farts
Who bare their bottoms in foreign parts
Of a world where war has already been
And have no need of a drunken scene?

Would you, Falstaff, have spread your grins,
Part humour, part cruelty, in inns
And places that only wanted quiet
From empty shouts and threatened riot?

Didn't you, Falstaff, yourself see a war
As an end to an end that had gone before?
Would you, with your beaker filled to the brim,
Have turned the streets to gauntlets grim

Where sober people walked in fear
And prayed that you be gone from here?
And when did you ever lurch with a leer
As if to destroy what was decent and clear?

Falstaff, when you were deep in your drink,
Did you ever conceive to place quill into ink
To ask why your bravery always yields
To the froth of the booze in your babbled green fields?

To Freud

Armies of steady scholars have been employed
Synthesizing that life of yours, dear Freud;
Historian you were, and a scientist too,
And, in your evolutionism, bore
Witness to what a man could feel and do
When undesired desirings fought and tore
His spirit, not invincible, into two;

You saw the unfruited values of the poor
Find recompense within the brood of war;
You saw the dramas pulled from history's tides,
From the era the Egyptians flouted Rome,
To the age when faith made men of faith take sides,
To the time when Universities near your home
Arose like Alexandrias as your guides;

From dramas like those, you chose the core and fruit
And, unrelenting, showed that, at the root
Of the fledgling vines called *character* and *depth*,
Freedom of thought comes, nurturing, too late
For most of us, who spend the breathy length
Of life being slaves, not conquerors, of fate;
In strength is freedom, and, in freedom, strength.

Seagull

A seagull's is the loudest cry
That potters down from out the sky
To land upon the fertile ground
And wake the weary with its sound;

While the waves lapped slowly along the shore,
Always the same, never lesser nor more,
One flighty gull, with its eagle's eyes,
Spotted a stillness that signaled a prize;

It circled the stillness with outstretched wings,
Looking for living, thus treacherous, things,
But its prize was not, it was solidly dead,
A body with eyes still intact in its head;

The seagull sank with its feet out-placed
On that body unfêted, but not disgraced.

One Hundred
Mood Studies

44

Absence

So, in sequestered absence, your intelligence
Will move you from me to a stranger place,
Where, all around you, men will work with diligence
To have my joy of gazing in your face;

And I will hide, a-wondering why fortitude
And work become so dull when you're not there;
A sort of mould or festering of attitude
Eats at my world, while I try not to care;

And, with your nurtured eyes that speak a literature
Of high cognitions, values, fears, and stress,
You cannot see the placid perfect portraiture
That I uphold in place of your caress;

And so I slide, through sleep, from day to day,
Knowing that soon you'll have to go away.

Arc

A broken arc: such was the wood that swung
Its broken way from side to side of the stream;
In the rain, it seemed a sodden molten hook
That gripped the rain that fell on the swollen brook.

A broken arc: such was the bridge, as it hung
With missing timbers and downward-slanting beam;
In the rain, it seemed like a single broken hook
Gripping the rain as it fell on the swollen brook.

A broken arc: such seems the life that clung,
Gripping to safety after the tarnished gleam,
After the hope had broken, after the look
Had drained to safety, and nobody dared to brook

A fling or a passion to mend the broken arc
Of a life devoted to art that was suddenly dark.

Argent

In argent, trimmed with deep metallic gold,
In-chiselled would be your beauty's endless rhyme;
How else, if not in precious solid fold,
Could I ensure that you will outlast time?

But gold seems hard, and silver over-rough;
Your face is soft and warm, as well as firm;
And all that placid is, lies there, enough
To cancel out what hardness bones affirm;

So, in a quieter mould, I pour your praise,
Away from metal's hard enamoured score;
Words will suffice to anchor you for days,
Nights, months, years, and aeons more;

And, in the quiet suffuse of letters' train,
I will incise your beauty and my pain.

Arms

Like arms, the lowlands lifted their trees to the sky,
Suppliant; begging like upthrusted stabs of a knife,
Their branches stretched upwards for sunshine and cried for
    new life;
Only the silence of voicelessness silenced their cry.

And am *I* life, if, like a tree, as supposed,
I also wish voice and, baffled, am driven to wonder
Whether to praise peace of marriage or, angered, to thunder
That sun I demand from feminine souls interposed?

So Nature goes, hegemony arch-dialectic
Of this-goes-with-that, while the endlessly curious warrior
Conquers with claw or acclaims the more, the merrier;
And the writer, bemused, opts for a tired analectic

Of "passion brings poison" and "peace is a long-lasting
    potion";
But poets disparage the peace that can poison emotion.

Asphodels

The asphodels beguile the languid air,
And sheaves of glowing flowers adorn the hills,
Gathering light from the sheaves of sunlight's glare
And flaming forth the gold of daffodils—

These are the colours that can fuse when mind
Flows, like an Arcady that does exist,
Into a unity of wills combined
To bring about a landscape cleared of mist.

Such landscapes form from fusions of men's minds
With women's, with the first providing breath
And pressure, the second architectural kinds
Of colour, both the bane of inner death;

But here I sit, surrounded by new snow,
Wondering whether I'll ever truly know.

Being

I feel you are sighing, and possibly dying, from out of my being;
It seems so surprising that, once we had met and then striven
To nurture the mutual hope that our meeting had given,
You ever should vanish from all my invisible seeing.

I felt, as if caught on the crux of a great comprehension,
That only within your embrace would I find a solution
To guilt that I never achieved what I could, absolution
From throes of unending unfinishedness, ending new tension,

And, in your balletic encompassing self, lay belonging,
Release from the long irritation of love unrequited,
A golden and poem-like end to a voyage benighted
And trapped in a fog of unfathomed ununderstood longing.

But now there's an unwanted ending; another has taken you;
And I am as guilty as if I had run and forsaken you.

Birds

Birds behaunt the paranoiac mind
As symbols of death about to pierce and peck,
And symbols of people's chatterings unkind.

Art also haunts the paranoiac mind;
Art shows each bird as black and spotlike speck
On a landscape none can see except the blind.

A sky can haunt the paranoiac mind;
A sky can be gold where fledged messengers fleck
The air to show where death has been defined.

Death also haunts the paranoiac mind;
Each blackish bird of death is built to wreck
Community when funerals are assigned.

All artists work, but seldom dare to troll
The birds and art and sky of Van Gogh's soul.

Blush

And now you run; I saw a passing blush
Fade and quickly light out across
Your quiet face; it's I who now must flush
All care and passion from my speech, and loss

Must now be frozen watchword of my verse.
It's silly, I suppose, to follow through
On quiet desires that augur for the worse
And only bring embarrassment to you;

And so, in a tailing off of sudden kind,
I write of how the glory of your eyes
Will sparken into life another mind
Who, younger, will yet win you, wooing wise;

But, though I know my heart must now relent,
I simply cannot write "all passion's spent."

Burden

It is too great a burden to be wise
And understand what dreaming underlies
This moderated verse, this tactful spate
Of sentences too pithy to be great;

That which is wise can spoil the pouring-spout
Of the ewer that lets one's gushing feelings out;
Heavy can rest the load of all that's mental
On the expression of what's more fundamental;

Black can seem a lovely sun in June
When love has been addressed, but stopped too soon;
Weighty can seem the clouds of southern seas
That merely signal sand and cooling breeze.

If I could move my overload of thinking …
No, that's no good, I'll merely dream of drinking.

Clothes

Today your clothes were pale, a silver blue
And blue of azure, and in sympathy
Your eyes took on a greyer sheen, and you
Seemed to be paler as you talked with me.

But talk we did, and there was open laughter
And an air emerged of quieter understanding;
Our talk was all of theories but, after,
All I recalled was how you looked when standing,

When, in the doorway's frame, you quietly stood
While I, intact with clarified conception,
Cognised that, though you seemed to be so good,
Your inner heart made goodness seem deception;

And yet the goodness clearly in your face
Served a clear aim; it neutralized disgrace.

Clouds

Lankly, the laggard clouds spread haggard drifts of rain
In hairlike white bestrung upon a background blue;
The raindrops fall in ones or twos, then hiss again
With a drumming as hundreds into thousands grew;

The lashing rain, that whips the leaves to underwhite,
Crashes in molten gold-drops on the grass; the cloud
That sheets the living blue and hides its lovely light,
Stands, in conquest over the land, as the raindrops crowd;

And the rose, so stark and strong in the summer's yellow air,
Now wilts, and cannot stir to shake the rain that flays;
Colour has gone, the rose, once flare, is now despair,
And the grass, once glare, is now greyed to a faded glaze;

And the rain pours on, and crushes the heart of the rose and the
    grass;
The rain is a grief, like a loss, as the summer days finish and pass.

Dark

I walk into the dark with you,
With you I want to stay;
Your slender hand that once was banned
Now holds me in its sway.

The night is light suffused with dark,
With lighter, tinting grey;
The night is light, but never quite
Develops into day,

So on we go, recalcitrant
To let our feelings play;
Our hands feel faint, we feel the taint
Of others in our way.

And all the night is like a darkened shroud
That falls on silence, calling out aloud.

Darkness

In what cool darkness lurks my verse?
It cannot pierce the light of loss,
So rolls encumbered, ponderous,
And tolls a ragged rhyme or worse.

How would your eyes retrieve its surge?
They would, in blessed satins, trap
The lineaments of its weave and nap,
And cataract its moansome dirge

To paean, praise of all you are,
If there were mercy in your look,
If you don't close me like a book,
If you don't spurn me from afar.

But who am I to chide your pride
When you, not I, were cast aside?

Dawn

In vain I execrate the dawn that lies,
Now primrose, on a budding bed of flowers;
Light that glows to full and blooms, then dies,
Contains more wishes (than real hopes) of hours

Spent in the passing fullness of your eyes.
A quickened glance, a fleeting fulsome burst,
And I dream that the dawns and quiet auroras rise
And fade away—the dreams have done their worst.

So dawns arise and fade at passing glances;
Hopes arise and fade as you go by;
The dawn illuminates, but day advances
Till sundry nothingnesses blot the sky;

Day, with its tawdry workaday and grey,
Darkens the dream and drives the dawn away.

Dawns

Are dawns but dreams untouched by imperfection?
How high the dawn can soar, unchained from learning,
Unspoilt by blame, unmoved by recollection
Of saddened hopes and slowly poisoned yearning!

How high it can soar, quite empty of birds singing,
Horizon untrammelled by trees, the total birth
Of yellow suffusing the fringes as sunlight, bringing
The radiant day, arousing all the earth!

And how one can mar that perfection, alluding
To blood in the veins of inebriate goddesses dying,
Re-decorating storm clouds, and, laughing, denuding
The gold with a knifescape of lovelight's denying!

Yes, how one can poison a dream with reality
Based on a potent, if partially formed, partiality!

Day

If I should find myself one day alone,
And a long, hard, bitter yoke of loneliness
Pressed on my shoulders down upon the bone,

Still I could never crawl, or try to surge
To claim my portion of your comeliness;
Because, although our hopes and minds converge

On a single range, a dream fulfilled of life,
Our ages speak that, as we grow and age,
Age would set up some deep and inner strife:

My hair would grey while yours grew thick and lush,
And, as my footsteps shortened with each stage,
Yours would step out; ongrowing age would crush,

With its damning slowness and all its darkening toll,
The tender fruit within our common soul.

Doles

Even the darkest doles of vice
The most inhibited entice,
And garner, in great gleanings wild,
The fascination of the child;

But in between those soulful yearnings,
Chidings, hidings, turnings, burnings,
Peace like a solemn thunder-toll
Encapsulates its quieter role,

And when with peace the tired eyes turn
To where the vicious yearn and burn,
They yearn as well for inner strife
For this is what delimits life.

And, with a yawn, the quiet mature
Despise themselves for being pure.

Dream #1

If dream there be that is not dreaming dark,
And light's as if of pleasure rich and stark,
Dappled with light like fields and orchards held
In a strong rich bowl of sunlight matte and gelled,
Such dream is only "if" and is not "is."

Yet, as the quiet straight landscapes roll on by,
Filling the void from earth unto the sky,
They do not seem to hold: they slide, quite fleet,
As if their image would my world make sweet
And fill my laden days with promises;

And so the dreams slide by, the days slide on,
The fields and rivers sing in unison,
And in their mirrored verdure lurks a hope;
But this I cannot hold, so only grope.

Dream #2

I fade, I float, I feed into a quiet paternal dream,
While unsown acres feed the willows of my age,
Dreaming, like bliss, of sundawns that barely seem to gleam;
I crown the acres of my verse with persiflage.

Is everything pretense? Can I not dream to be like you,
Young with the gentle glances of your fathers round you,
And trapped in behaviour-worlds that never seem to strike you
As over-quiet, because desire does not surround you?

Into the mourning halls of deaths that never happened,
Out onto the mountains of lusts that were fulfilled,
Stare the outwitted bards whose brains were quite out-weaponed
By simple eyes of girls that cleansed those brains and thrilled

A better verse into being, with a purer clarion,
While verses meant to conquer decomposed like carrion.

Dreamings

Back and forth the dreamings go
As if they spoke of fire and want
Bedimming in your absence, so
Need firing from a poet's font;

Then every line pretends a dream
Except the one that, since it meant
The truth, reigns in my mind supreme,
The dream I let you go—you went

Over a cliff into—where? The air?
I do not know, except that I
Did not go frantic with despair
But merely sighed a lover's sigh:

Gone, she is gone, thought I aloud,
But felt no longer poet-proud.

Dust

I have a drive to dream you into dust,
To play, within my mind, a play of you,
Projecting, on my mental screen, a view
Of you cavorting, with effective lust,

So as to urge defeat of what you see,
My under-embodied superficial mind,
A twister of scorpion tricks and blind
To when you really are desiring me.

Hints? I am hopeless at their taking;
I cannot pass the salt unless asked clearly.
Winks? I do not know when you are faking,
So, socially polite, pretend I'm nearly

Ready to stay with you, while putting on
My overcoat, hastening to be gone.

Earth

Is it then not enough to simply love,
To simply know that, on this chequered earth,
Exists a soul who does not need to prove
Herself an equal or to weigh her worth,

Who does not need to shine or primp her smile,
Or wear immaculate *maquillage*, or hide
Her golden eyes beneath a veil of guile,
But simply look with simple unfeigned pride,

Who does not need to speak, except to say
A simple strong opinion, born of right,
And does not need to masquerade, or play
An archery of feigned and female fright,

Who does not need, in other words, to do
A single thing to prove she is for you?

Eye #1

How gleams the mortal eye when thoughts of death
Rear in a blear horizon to the mind!
And how the brightened interplay of breath
Zones, in a mood, all lovers intertwined!

And how these deep thoughts of love and death and life
Scatter when broken on a moment drear!
And how in a land of deadened leaves does strife
Enact its play when winds blow stark, and shear!

And how, from excitement, do the thought-waves hurl
Like waves upon the blockwall of the soul!
And how, from attraction to each passing girl,
Do sheaves of Art grow high and hale and whole!

And so, in apostrophisings part pedantic,
Roll on the words of a would-be late Romantic.

Eye #2

Now, with a clear, unconvoluted eye,
I see the mild amusement of the crowd
At how I let my softness lead me, by
The hand, into a sobbing out aloud.

Too bad I was not more like Don Juan,
Who would have been beloved for what he did
If jealous rivalry had not outrun
His girl's desire; caressing, at her bid,

Is fine for one, but not for two or more—
A woman's pride is stronger than her flesh—
But, had I followed sense, the outraged roar
Of virulent deception would enmesh

Me, darkly, in a downfall like a Don;
At least, that is the sane opinion.

Eyes #1

For why is it your eyes of deepest brown
Fill me with thoughts of a nature always serious,
So that my hopes are inwardly dashed down
And trap my verses in an iron imperious?

It is, of course, the fact that you are all
I ever sought out in a female form;
Your looks, your mind, your gentle voice appal
Me with their full agreement with the norm

I set within myself of an ideal
Of womanhood; and, though I know both whores
And female saints, they cannot steal
From you the sheer reality that bores,

Like a remorseless drill, through all my dust
Of disillusionment and dour distrust.

Eyes #2

I'm desperate to drink within your eyes,
But, if they fill with fear as I approach,
I worry that I take you by surprise,
Moving so fast that Eros frowns reproach,

Then I move back and stare down at my book;
You are too young—no, no, I am too old,
And, with my hardened lusting for your look,
I desecrate the adult power I hold.

But when the quietness of your absence comes,
And I am driven back into my verse,
My need to know you better overcomes
All fear my desperation is perverse;

My desperation is as simply true
As all the beauty that envelops you.

Eyes #3

Chat, chat till, in your eyes,
I found renewed, to my surprise,
The fateful state I entered in
When first I felt your whitened skin

And when, as the sun fell cold in March,
We stood beneath a doorway's arch,
And I took your hand to say goodbye,
And found, instead, I had to try

To hold you tight with just one hand,
Because I felt the countermand
Not just to shake your hand, polite,
But clasp you, grasp you, hold you tight—

When, as I say, the sun fell cold,
I crossed the line from brave to bold.

Façade

You wrote, I wrote back: all seems to be quite jolly,
And yet this great façade leaves me depressed;
I wish to see you, but my fear of folly
Leads me to crush my feelings unexpressed;

And yet, when I see them written in these lines,
And flinch to think how future minds may mock
At the vast rift 'twixt thought and outer signs,
I feel I am a boat that starts to rock;

And I dreamed, last night, I drifted far and wide,
I'd lost my hotel's name in wild New York;
All that seemed solid seems to quail beside
The bobbings of my feelings like a cork:

I cannot move, I cannot retrogress,
I dare not love you more, and cannot less.

Farewell

To say farewell—to break, with a single word,
A net of quiet concupiscence that cast,
Within its wordy weave, all that would last
From thoughts that were written, never to be heard—

To say farewell—to break imagination
With a single stroke, fracturing works of weeks,
Turning them into ephemera, old antiques
From a truthful forge of hope and pure creation—

To say farewell—to damn with a single sound
Night after night of dreaming, and the days
Of waiting for your footfall, and your gaze
That told me, in a moment, I had found

What years of search had hidden from my eyes:
To say farewell would end these lines with lies.

Feelings

For feelings do what feelings have to do:
There is no forcedness to a genuine love
But something black, implacable, and few
There are who are not felled by fears that rove

Unnervingly across the paths of needs.
These fears strike deep: supposing that she cries
For a stronger, less impassioned man, who feeds
Her need to be stable, making all your sighs

Echo on pages emptily and die
In a quiet neurotic grave of love undone?
What if she flinches, hardly stirred or moved

By your hard unyielding ardour? Are you loved,
Or merely spurned as the over-sensitive one
Who, being in love, had not the wit to lie?

Gains

Tell me, what fit and follied gains perverse
Could come of faint relief of this my tension,
To see you smile, and realize that the worse
Is yet to come should I lose your attention?

I see them now, bright youths with jaws of bone,
Clever, and rich in stocks and real estate;
I see them now, young graduates who alone
With beards and glasses understand the great;

I see them now, the ones who speak of farms
And the idyll of a rural bungalow;
I see them now, with their loving gentle arms
Taking you in their clasp, and I cry, no—

But feebly, for I cannot hold you fast.
I am the first to know I'll be the last.

Glances

Glances quick, and sudden fatal falls,
Are the conglomerate entities of love;
And yet the honest looks you give me prove
That this is not an accident that stalls

On the slightest shove of nonchalance, or steers
A vanishing arc in the quelling of desire,
Or lapses into loathing if the fire
Should be drenched out by morals or by fears;

Your honest looks, yet laced with youthful smile,
Steer me instead to a fantasy of fate
In which we share a future reprobate
Because enmixed with treachery and guile;

And this I do not think that I could bear,
So all my dreams, I think, I must forswear.

Gloom

Through what deep-thwarted gloom does crass perception
Make, of gold carpets, dullness full of fluff,
With the soft silver of antiques a crude deception,
Hardness where softness itself would mean enough?

This darkness would twist, bewilder itself into honesty,
Be pure and light and hopeful of happiness, were this
So to bewilder my mind that darkness were travesty,
Veiling a lightness redolent of a kiss,

But, in rendering gloom that I have lost you,
All seems perjury-light, mornings seem hollows,
Sunshine feels always cold, and the breezes of spring
Seem to deny that summer the spring always follows:

Let there be light, the tulips seem to sing;
But light is just physics that the seasons bring.

Gold

Observe how gold and silver can be lost,
Mired in volcanic deep or holocaust,
And tarnished can be the silver bought at cost,
Melted can be the gold, or jewelers exhaust

Their frantic stocks of preciousness, and turn
To chalices inscribed with praise of you
And, in a usurer's glee, defile and burn
What monuments were made of your purview;

Words are better, for they force their way
Upon the mind, and last in fathers' songs
To children, and in odic lines that weigh
The past's inheritance of rights and wrongs;

So breathe in beauty from her beauteous eyes;
Truth may fool, but beauty never lies.

Hand

It is quite rarely that you show your hand,
While, in my somber conflict, here I stand,
Feeling an exile in a foreign land
Where fountains play, uncaring that I'm banned;

And, as the leaves so rarely move, revealing
The verdant fruits the flowers are concealing,
You only rarely show me what you're feeling,
While I persist in outwardly appealing.

I could say, as I did before, that you are hard
And I am soft, snow-like, because I'm barred
From doing more than singing love ill-starred,
And boring you by claiming I am scarred;

But none of these are more than gleams of thought
Hiding the truth: I let you go when caught.

Impostor?

Am I impostor to be polyamorous
And yet protest my ardour to your face?
Life is too short for playful bigamies,
And yet too long to live with *no* disgrace;

If I see others, at a fête or fair,
Or spot a distant hem, trying not to stare,
And yet still track its eye-ascendant flare,
Its skirt weaving waywardness everywhere

Along the path-lined pavements of the street,
With all the men pretending not to care,
I feel that a wall of worthiness discreet
Protects the wondrousness of those who dare

Reveal, in petticoated walk, more that speaks of life
Than does a hero or his super-virtuous wife.

Jealousy

Jealousy has the mood of a sky
Whose grey is mixed with jade:
It conjures a willingness to die
When all its debts are paid.

The sky sounds a sigh of distant hurt,
Because, at the time, what seemed a hope
Was merely the pleasantry of a flirt
Who dangled you on her psychic rope;

The sigh has not reached thunder yet;
The clouds are tinged with a vacant hue;
The sun, though red, has not yet set;
The grey of the sky has blurred to blue.

Only when rains begin to storm
Will you feel your heartbreak loom and form.

Knowledge

Your beauty, not your knowledge, thinnish is;
And yet it overwhelms your mirror's frame;
There is an end to mystic lands and fantasies,
But knowledge can't outdo a beauty's fame.

Mountains may rise and oceans fall, and tides
May apprehend the rainings' winnowing sands,
But always fixed, so long as time abides,
Will be the beauty that your fame commands;

It matters not if blue or brown your eyes,
Or colour hair, or how endusk'd your skin—
What should stand firm across the centuries
Is that your time-locked beauty stay within

A verse like this, which proves, like all the arts,
That Art with beauty, not with knowledge, starts.

Land

As placid as the land that stretches, stalls, and stops
From halt to halt, hedge to hedge, copse to copse,
Onward for halting miles, endlessly broken by crops
But linked from eastern cliff to western forest wall,

Placid unhindered by passion, peaceful unhampered by grief,
The loveliness of your addressing surpasses my weary belief,
And to steal you away from your youth would ennoble me into a
    thief;
The feelings steal into the landscape and slowly incorporate all:

Placid the fields in the glow of the sunset's disconsolate light,
Placid the stares of the cattle as grasses turn grey as the night
Placidly drapes all the landscape to counter the evening's flight,
And the stars, symbols of sadness, have not yet pierced its pall;

Your placidity comes from unknowing; you never have needed to
    feel
Reciprocity born of my longing, a longing I dare not reveal.

Landscape

The slow, quiet fields of the landscape loom,
Fade, flit, and zoom,
As the train lengthens the countryside
By miles and shortens time to a morning's ride;

The sky moves faster than the sun
That seems to run
Arcwise across the window's frame
In a blatant blaze like a bright white flame.

Capture the time, a moment's quiet
In one's lifetime's riot
Of over-emotion never quite blending
With easy release; covet a happy ending;

And fill your private space with ease
As your train trundles and sidles between tall trees.

Light

If light be light, illuminating dark,
And wild light be whiter than a spark
Against the black, dazzling the black to show
Itself as poor and dim, bereft of glow,
It is not light I yearn for, save as brain;
It's colours that I want to see again.

And if dark be black without a single hue,
A simple nothing, emptiness of view,
Referring, in quiet jealousy, to white
As nearest colour to its offspring, light,
It is not dark I yearn for, save as place
To hide myself from mental self-disgrace.

No—colours would be as harmony on hills
When springtime's stream with melody refills.

Lines

"Though fine the finer lines upon your face,
And frail the further follies of your heart,
How could I not upon their beauties place
A kiss, were I allowed to play that part?"

Thus write I, for, in fantasies bereft
Of all fruition, must I hide and sigh;
The world goes spinning round me, but I'm left
In a sort of epic hollow, life a lie;

Nothing is right, yet everything is right;
In a cool sweet order, Nature plays her play;
Were I to have you, who can know what night
Could on us hap-descend one summer day?

Thus write I onwards, wondering if I'm mad
To ponder so on what I never had.

Man

I know a man who, one time, beauty spurned
On moral grounds, a quickly made decision,
Then felt a grief as if that beauty burned,
While beauty faded into imprecision;

No more could he the sunset's growing gold
See burden the sky with symmetry of black
Or feel that natural beauty smiled; it told
Instead of loss that never would come back;

And there, while evening's russet clouds unrolled,
And stark grey birds called final nighttime shrills,
And the night wind sighed and whistled onward cold,
As a final blackness hid the daffodils,

Beauty for him was gone, gone like a star
Seen by him once, then fled to darkness far.

Marginality

Although in marginality a compromise
Promises "will be" and shuns off blocks of "never,"
Lines that re-echo from hills will never rise
From the adoption of "it won't be," ever;

So I must claim to pretend to hope, and bastion,
From fainter hopes and compromises, hopefulness,
All shrouded by the faintly hopeless question
Of whether what is only dreamed is emptiness;

"No!" cries poetry, "I am the *living* dream;
My subtle acres score from hope reality;
I can across my soaring hills redeem
Emptiness from thought and give it quality;

"I can, from a dried-out vessel, vintage take
And from it new originations make;

"And from my song of hope, borne up by arms
Super and vented from my songster's charms,
I can elect to paint, in pictures furious,
The magical, the golden-charmed, the curious,
The alchemists' chant of rock made into gold,
The overflow of allegory's fold,
The oratory of great marble rare,
Ceilings awash with upheld cupids fair,
Nights made soft brown by Nature's subtle brush,
Days made soft blue by dawn's betraying blush,
Winters made fourfold warm by blooms of sun
And joined to summers in reunion."

And I, who painted, from my words, regret,
Seek, in its light, new words to buoy me yet.

Mind #1

Cold and calm, thy neutral mind
Flavours numbers, graphs, and charts
With equal reason, reason blind
To all the turmoil of the arts;

And in repose, thy paler face
Seems like a neuter in this pause;
But what simplicity of grace
Lends a new poetry to thy cause!

So on through neutral, pale, and white
Sing the pure colours of thine eyes;
And I in the workday world must fight
The urge to quietly rhapsodise.

So meetings go, from day to day;
Will work give way one day to play?

Mind #2

No outer mind, no other person's aims,
Should penetrate this armour of our souls
That, self-perpetuating inner goals,
Raises the high proud spectre of our fames;

For I see you, and in your inner mind
I see a quiet prosperity of love;
And in my mind you find an equal trove
For inspiration of a newer kind;

And so, in equal movement, we adopt
A kind of symmetry of equal gain
That reinforces secret inner smiles

That we have meant so much; the thought beguiles
That, up to now, there's been no inner pain,
And all the pain of past romance has stopped.

Moment

And in a moment's heaven of a joke,
Our eyes met, fused, and all the hidden grey
That filled my mind, until it nearly broke,
Fused to an azure, blowing all away.

And in an equal moment of control,
Back we re-fell to earth, and talked and worked,
Darkening heaven to a thunder-roll
Beneath which hopes and hollownesses lurked.

And we went on in talk, and fused to smile
Goodbye, but made a future pledge to meet
Within two days, and said goodbye, all while
I wondered if I ought to beat retreat.

And this is real; each solid line and rhyme
Have a fixed fusion anchored in real time.

Moments

In moments of bleak conflict, such as these,
My fervour is as silent as the breeze
That blows, unfeeling, through the standing trees;
My feelings waver wanly like the wind.

And if I hope to find that candour frees
My conscience from my questions and my pleas,
My heart retorts and simply disagrees;
Remorselessly it says that I have sinned.

But what is Sin, and what's a man if he's
A craven beggar even on his knees
Before the Nature he can never please
And whose commandments no one can rescind?

No, Nature will win at last, but at the cost
Of endless wondering at what I've lost.

Muse

Although the Muse lends softness to the tune,
The words themselves are loud and quite relentless,
A never-ceasing threnody, quite endless,
Of loss that seems more lasting than the moon;

And all the stars that shine a-down, resplendent,
Are faint and quiet when seen as merely nature;
Each grief and loss of love is a creator
Of stellar inward stars, on grief dependent;

And every inward star shines like a union
Of mind and hapless memory encaptured
On skies of black, with hopes and griefs enraptured,
So fused are they with moments of communion;

And, of these stars, one shines so deadly bright
That it can burn the daylight from my sight.

Night #1

The night that walks, on open harbours drear,
Captures in hands the incapacitate;
The creaking of the masts against the night
And the clash of tinny wires against the night,
Halter a clamour too precipitate;
Night holds, in hands, the vanquished ultra-clear;

And, where pure reason falls beneath the spell
Of passion that enlarges all the sphere
Of possible things, and, into clearer light,
Thoughts meld, suffusing, into deeper light,
The night turns back on dark foreboding fear,
And turns to a world where clarities dispel

Lightness and darkness, fusing into one
A simple, if unsaid, communion.

Night #2

When, as in further darkening night, the races
Of wind-lashed cataracts and quiet streams
Act suddenly calm, deadening places
Where quick-and-full meet slow-and-calm like dreams,

The facts of what you can and cannot do
To all I am lash me like a wave;
The concentration of my thought seems true
But stark expression outwardly seems brave;

Were there no faith to block my outward lines
Then would they flow more freely than a flood;
Instead they are honed, defined in sharp designs,
Trammelled, leashed, with more of brain than blood;

But, in this hard affected verse, my goal
Is merely to rebuild my battered soul.

Night #3

Although the night draws down her sable veil
Like a great robe of black upon the sun,
Hiding in darkness all the wordings stale
Of promises unkept and hopes undone,

The darkness is a sort of cheat, a thief
Who comes, sequestered in a family guise,
To rob believers of their dear belief
That no things matter more than lovely eyes

And stark romance of oceanic bliss;
But this great night descends upon us all,
Making a cheap harassment of a kiss,
And a mockery of every madrigal.

Still, such nights end when virtue is forsaken
And, out of daydreams, deeper truths awaken.

Night #4

A tardy night that stands untaint by day,
Like cycles of Octobers spread by heat,
Each a wet darkness haunt by laden grey,
A night that stands persistent and replete;

Is all this darkness really born of want,
A never-ending suppliance of need,
That scars bright summer days to empty cant,
And takes all watchword glory from each deed?

The night wears on, the thoughts roll wanly on.
Can I never retrace the steps from one great grief,
And somehow bring a sunshine's orison
To paint a brightness onto grey relief?

Once darkened, once dampened, never can the soul
Recover without fracture of the whole.

Note

Now drifts a starker note, a far more serious note:
The past that went before we met was known without you,
The futures that will fill the future years without you
Were, and forever will be, tides of years that float

Without you. Will there be crescents then of moonlit nights,
Or suns that shine like present mornings all upon you,
Or shine on high like the high empyrean blue upon you,
Or golden days that shower the dawn's pre-sentient lights

Upon you? And will, in those long absences, my soul
Find more to say, or less to say, or naught about you,
And find, with not a shred of effort, gold about you,
And will I find, with stifled heart, that words still roll

About you, so that I cannot stop and vaguely stare
At the hollowness of my books because you are not there?

Nothing

Now all that was and will be, ended is,
And nothing but arch moral stands and mocks;
Solicitudes are racking penuries,
And goodness grins in goodness from the stocks;

An overwhelming ethical "right attitude"
Glows from the arch incompetence of my act;
A redolence of never-ending quietude
Retails the final nature of your pact;

And I must in gloom begin to seem in zest,
Be teller of tales, a wit so debonair,
Social must I become, while in my chest
Sobbing and weeping contend in dumb despair;

And I must, in ever-perfect rectitude,
Fight the instilment of you within my blood.

Opportunity

He had awaited the opportunity
To un-admire what made Miss X look great,
And re-admire, with importunity,
Her intellect, to which he could relate;

A virtual life, in a virtuous death becalmed,
Was in his mind, on that silly summer day,
When he tried, in her mentality embalmed,
To forge a mental mating that would stay;

He thought she smiled on hearing his endeavour
Free to remain unfettered by her eyes;
He swore, no tight embraces ever
Would sully their non-romantic enterprise;

But, when she demurred, he abandoned his silly scheme;
He'd learned that *he* was not as pure as he might seem.

Pain

I knew a pain like this, quite long ago;
We fought, she flirted, flew, and, pouting, parted;
And I knew then that pangs are pains that go
And come when one is cowed and broken-hearted;

And, as I look and as we talk, I see
The now enpallored sculpture of your face,
And your fine eyes searching for a life to be,
And put myself within your puzzled place;

I curse both youth and follied age-pretension
That crash upon the hurdles of "What if?"
What if we both were free of all this tension
And, single-hearted, simply followed life?

For life is the entity that stirs my pain
When I see you and see my youth again.

Pearldom

I never touched you once, nor felt the pure
White pearldom of your skin, and never knew
An unadornèd *effleurage* from you;
Only a lacy hope my dreamings bore;

And now I dare not dream, and all the air
Must vanish in a quiet recalcitrance,
A simple fade; and all my remonstrance
Is empty colour, hope no longer there;

And yet this nothing is a better state;
There is a faded fervour in its light,
A sort of quiet Nirvana of the night
With not a single star illuminate;

And, even now, this nothing shows a gleam
That all I dreamed of was no idle dream.

Poems

If I beholden had been unto thee
For poems only, O unwitting muse,
My friends and colleagues would have labeled me
As one who science *or* art could freely choose;

But that is not fair; I'm driven to art;
"Choice" is not a word even in play;
For thou it was who coaxed my longing heart
Into turning a night-time's liturgy to day;

Thou it was, who, while I silently wrote
My silent sonnets only for *mine* ears,
Crested my verse to living antidote
To loss of thee and to my growling fears

That, were I to show my reverence for thee,
I would be punished for idolatry.

Quietude

If, with my calm Giovannic quietude,
I seem to skirt the ruthless and the rude,
Do not pretend that I am fleeing Truth—
I only guard the plenitude of Youth;

I only keep the crest aloft of Drive;
I only steer to where my longings thrive;
I only stash a secret part of Heaven
Into my cropped Earth, its rise to leaven;

I only seek what never had been lost
Had action not been compromised by cost;
Only in dream can I my Real inhale,
And only in rhyme its phantasms regale;

I am a turgid clot who crawls the ground
Between the walls of Enigma and Sound.

Rain

Rain does not mean storm, nor darkness rage;
A flying cloud that hides the morning's light
Can be a bitter foreshadow of age,
Or just a memory's sadness recondite;

And morning still can sing and sign the trees
With greenness singing pastorals of life;
The cloud that passes only stirs a breeze,
Bringing to peace a foreshadow of strife;

But the morning blazes bluer when the grey
Has gone, dispelled by sunlight's stronger glow;
And, in the radiant sunshine of the day,
Night and dark starlights bow their heads and go;

But a deep, cold chill of dark experience past
Warns that such dawnlight cannot always last.

Rue

Mild rue, mild rue at what I did not do
Makes ruminations rumble on forever;
I could make clouds, make rainfall, from my rue,
And tumbling downpours could become a river.

But on it must go, must life, and so must I,
And not fall, faltering, in my lonely way;
But every time I see you passing by
And watch the warm sequester of your sway,

And the high beauty of your cheeks, and note
How your hair bestirs your lovely neck, and seems
In a quiet ecstatic air to quietly float,
Appendage to yourself and to my dreams,

I simply sit, and write these lines, resigned,
And do not know for whom they are designed.

Sadness #1

Sadness appals the lightened heart
And cruelty brings tears;
Children know the harsh of both,
And so do those of years;

The fine upstanding youth of yore
Bore cleavers, axes, swords;
The children wept to see such fun
And the elders weighed their words;

Sadness appals the lightened heart,
And the weight that woe can weave,
Burden the heart, and naught of light
Can hearten those who grieve,

Except in those who happiness have known
Because, in childhood, happiness was sown.

Sadness #2

It may have been that, were I young and free,
No sadness would be graven on my art;
And when you looked into my eyes, you'd see
Bright youth, not sadness, graven on my heart;

But I am older, and the graven years
Have stamped their fledgling forbears on my mind;
I see too well your young and tremulous fears
That I shall love too hard if you are kind;

I see where, carved on archways of your soul,
Hopes of horizons gleam, unflaked by cares;
And castles built upon my lifetime's whole
Cannot be seared by younger beauty's flares;

But always your lovely eyes illuminate
The turrets that my dreams have forged of late.

Sadness #3

A sadness when you leave and I must wait
Till further meetings, sets a furbished sigh
On the happiness I feel obliged to state,
That fills me with rueful joy when you pass by;

And all of the rue that fills my silent hours,
And makes me so serious in my normal life,
Seems to take flight in times that are just ours
And no one else stands sentinel to strife;

But, were I free and young to shout my fill
Of how your being fills my mind to sate,
Then would I surely lose to overkill,
And see you shrink from pleas importunate;

So it is best, perhaps, that you and I
Keep at arm's length, and yet see eye to eye.

Sadness #4

A sadness that welled up like tears
Suddenly struck me, melted me low,
And all the long hurt of younger years
Seemed to remount me from below:

The dazing whirl of dating and waiting,
The phones that did not ring, the rain
That always fell in spring, frustrating
Hopes of hiding from the pain,

And now, the pain of being too old,
The way my workday never ends,
The griefs that future years unfold,
The fading peace I show my friends—

This sadness and these views betray
The truth I never dare display.

Sky

The sky is leaden grey; with cold
It self-same shivers in the clouds,
And a wild wind springs a hundredfold
To blow the cobwebs into shrouds;

Winter is waste, it plays no part
In writing all the greying lines
That tell the story of a heart
That cannot do what greed assigns;

The sky is sunny, I feel sad;
The sky is dark, I feel secure;
Only a youth who knows no bad
Can praise the sky for being pure;

No, when you get older, all there is
Is heart devoid of mysteries.

Sin

What sign of sin or good is inner pain
That seems transcendent, though it can be pushed
Rapidly from our chests, through act of brain,
And seems so slight it's easy to be crushed?

These moments tell us what our minds do not:
Sadness when others round us laugh with mirth,
An irkdom with domestic joys, a spot
Of boredom at the thought of a new birth,

Envy at marriages, glee at discontents,
All these unsound emotions speak the truth,
As does that inner pain that speaks a sense—
The sense that age does not go well with youth;

But now it's all flat and neutral like a sea,
As neutral as an inner pain can be.

Smile #1

Thy lightened smile, that rivals idolize,
Smiles on a me emburdened by my longing;
I do not dare to smile, my serious eyes
Would hurt the fervent lightness of your hope,
And their sequestered earnestness would blight
The reasonings of future viewed as light;

But if I should, with sudden lines, surprise
The weight I place on you by my belonging
In mind to you, and ease it with demise
Of seriousness, a mirrored overlap,
Jaunty and nonchalant and debonair,
So that it weighed not woeful, but as air;

Then would I be betrayer of my craft
And fear the cachinnation as you laughed.

Smile #2

An argent smile, an urgent smile
That drives all woes away,
Shows just the sort of healthy guile
Of hopeful lovers' play;

A blazing smile, a glazing smile
Of utter high communion
Shows just the sort of lovers' wile
That forces both to union;

A goldened smile, a boldened smile
That flashes through the air
Shows a sophisticated style
Of fusion formed from flair;

But, when your gentle smiles have gone,
A subtle happiness lives on.

Snow #1

Gentle but steady, snow is falling, palling the wilderness,
Lending a snow-white softness to dark and stapled fences,
Covering the dry garrets of the grasses with seemly furriness,
White and entrenched, resembling the rigours of all your
    defenses.

I fight with a mental sword in my hand against the surprise
Of your flight; I cower, bearing a sombre mental spear
To stop and deflect the pure iron that shines and reflects in your
    eyes;
I spring up again, cursing and trampling on all my fear.

But rigour falls and on the unmelting encapsulation
Of your objections to me, a blandness falls like snow,
Covering, drenching, drowning my innermost sense of negation
While you remain hard and unmoved. I sense I have nowhere to
    go;

The soft and hard unite like snow falling on metal,
The snow my plea, and you the iron on which it may settle.

Snow #2

The snow falls and is over-powerful;
It isolates me from the things I see.
Outside is whisper-itching cold; in here,
In a room where warmth and light are running free,
I see through the window cold and falling snow
And quietly question whether I should go

Into that laden day of snow so plentiful
That ice and snow have clouded every tree;
The snow is not inviting, and I fear
The clutch of its clamorous cold surrounding me.
I look though the window at white-lit grass and lawn,
Hunched like a baby hare against a dawn;

I look through the window at white-lit lawn and grass
Hunched till the snow grow stiff and fade and pass.

Strike

A mail strike, well then, nothing comes amiss;
All's safe, because thou dost not need to say
That thou hast thus done these or that or this
And I can think, she'll write another day;

But this is daft, I know it, thou must know,
That every day my mailbox empty lies
Is like a landscape where no breezes blow
Or an empty church devoid of mysteries;

And I should feel more cheerful, running here
Or there, as if one letter more or less
Were nugatory in my hemisphere,
A non-event, a simple nothingness;

But, if this daftness won't evaporate,
All letters will arrive too late, too late.

Summer

As summer's dawn gave signal of the day,
So the descending evening signals night,
And the engendered fading of the light
Signals the slow retrenchment of our play;

And, as your lowered eyelids flicker null,
And my mind on my own work focuses again,
All that we thought seems past and gone; but then,
As I wait to be accused of being dull,

I resurrect a semblance of your eyes;
I find they hold me fast in azure ropes
Of fine suffused armaments of praise,

Fettering, fast, amazing happy days
In those garnered times when both of us had hopes
That what seemed fancies were not simply lies.

Sunlight

The sunlight falls and over-decorates the flowers
With light exuberant; tulips burst full flowered,
Seizing, in quadruple light, the sun and dazzling it;
Grass, in unhaltered green, seems radiant to the eye;

But alternations of the dark and sunlit hours
That mark your living absence seem to have sown and soured
Time with a sort of soft refulgent glass; I sit
Surrounded by sunlight; but sunlight seems to pass me by;

The tulips seem darker; their yellow petals' brightness cowers
Before the onset of my dusk; the rains have showered
The brilliant grass with a sort of saddened fog; writ
Over the garden is a faded glory; the reason why

Is simple: you are not here, so all of my perception
Seems like a mocking mist, beauty a distant deception.

Sunshine

If I were now to say that sunshine bloomed
From every smile that blossomed from your eye,
I would be caught as poet reined and groomed
Who could not find a better song to sigh;

Yet it *is* as if flowers grew sundry in my mind
And yearned to catch the sunlight's nectared vein;
Each smile you give is like a light designed
To penetrate each fibre of my brain;

And I *do* feel sunlight pouring through my verse
As if each word were honed from sunlight fine,
And the slow recurrence of the cloudscape's curse
Caps like conjecture each question of a line;

So the sunlight fades, but memories stay bright;
Your eyes are nurture for a greater light.

Temptation

Temptation: am I traitor for not moving
To press into caresses what I felt,
For you, before, unfelt, my act of proving
That age did not suit reason, dumbly dealt

A blow to all that forced us close together?
It was not mean, but kind; how could I let
You fall, self-falling, in a trap whose tether
Held a self-defeating sort of net?

But now, the hunter, I am lost and aching;
Could not some hopes for both be grasped and seized,
Out of a close-knit closeness of our making,
A hope of hope for pleaser and for pleased?

So: close togetherness stands cold, renounced,
And I feel traitor, fit to be denounced.

Thought #1

Betray no thought of mine, lest a betrayal
Of all my inward forces fuses to farce
This single-minded portrait of portrayal
Of all your beauty caught in poet's verse;

Leave me in freedom, freedom to portray
What might arise if I were only yours
For a day of single miniature, a day
Enlivened by a freedom that abjures

Danger for freedom to paint, and tactlessness
For utter and free unbridledness of my pen,
And solitude for now-togetherness,
And "Never!" for a loud resounding "When?"

Such freedom I only dream of, but I do,
Yet scarcely dare to hope my dream comes true.

Thought #2

The darkened thought that only a negation,
A nothing, will emerge from all this verse,
And mental exercise, incarceration
Of perfection, and the hope that nothing worse

Than nothing comes from all this verbalese
On the loveliness of your eyes and all the jet
Half-Eastern blackness of your hair—all these
Are all that all my dreaming's door will let

Escape into a nature independent;
And why? If all I gain is just for naught,
Why should I spend a fortune's time resplendent
Reconquering you with wares of speedlight thought,

When all I get are pages black and white,
Portraits of a passion half contrite?

Ugliness

Men can make art from even ugliness,
And carve, with horned hands, a lovely moon
From a rack or pillory—that is, unless
They're on it, praying for pity to come soon;

That is why art can never pay the price
That evil asks; art must, if art's to live,
Resist its tendency to sacrifice
The meaning to the beauty it can give;

Art must think large and sweep across the dross
Of blackish prejudice and careless cant;
It must distil a truth from every loss,
And draw a lesson, not a gloating rant,

From every victory, conquest, or success:
Sublimity must outweigh pleasantness.

Veil

How dark the veil through which no sunlight shines—
Pierced would be the mocking lace of black
Were a bright ray itself to pierce the lines
Of wicked night; but nothing shines to crack

The dark unpierced black; light vanished is,
And a mocking veil hangs thick across the face
Of mischief fused with fear; all mysteries
Seem set afree by knowledge of disgrace,

Shame, and the wicked hating blazing eye
Of treachery unbleached by worth; light
Vanished is; but lost, within the dye
Of black enmeshed with dark, enfeebled night

Hangs weakly; and stars that vanished into redolence,
Leave their quiet traces on a quiet malevolence.

Vein

Is there a vein that deep within me will not out?
Can I express all thoughts but one, the one that says
That I will never live with freedom free from doubt
If I ignore the truth of all these fantasies?

You came to see me; your hair was newly cut and brown;
"It's *really* nice," I said and threw, within those sounds,
Two years of admiration I could not keep down;
But, deep within, my youth within felt further bounds;

For were I now, with levity non-circumspect,
To take your hand and walk with you about the town,
How could I hide the grey with which my beard is flecked?
How could I play my old man's sense of conquest down?

I cannot; for I fear the deeper hidden thought
That, if I let you go, all instinct counts for naught.

Verse

Why, writing verse to others, do I feel
Unfaithful to the splendid part of me
That you alone preserves as being the real
And only meritor of poesy?

Why, when confronted with the eyes and smiles
And wonderful warmth of others, do I try
To wreathe their minds with verse that reconciles
Me to your loss but somehow leaves me dry?

And why, though I know that I am truly blessed
In having love that holds me firm and true,
Do I persist in wishing I caressed
A pliant and more freely smiling you?

It is because I have two souls within:
One that wants love, the other wants to win.

Virtue

Am I then mad, your virtue to decry
While hours and days and months go passing by
And I wait, half encumbered by delay
As hour fades into hour, day into day?

Do not decry impatience, let it stand;
It holds our selves together like a hand;
And, in the darkening winter days ahead,
Do not decry, but stand alert instead—

Alert to hold me back when I am free
To throw my fettered forfeits in thy fee
And give you all I have that you may be
Unfettered by a too impatient me;

Impatience is the watchword of my need,
And marks the words that overshade the deed.

Warmth

What warmth is this? What sun creeps upward glowing?
How can new landscapes form when all is done
And a quiet garden stands in place of all the flowing
Streams of a nature's forgone union?

Maybe quiet glow speaks raptures new to Time,
Still-to-be-felt oblivions from pain,
Still-to-be-written remnants of new rhyme,
And still-to-be-heard musics in new strain;

Or maybe the end is here, quiet tone of peace,
In whose sweet arms all pains and hurts subside,
And who, in quiet consiliate release,
Leaves us at peace with those who cannot bide;

Or maybe the quiet is foretaste of the end:
A lover not, but still a feeling friend.

Wastes

The wastes of lake and field and wood unfold,
And spread a waste between the distant places
Where you and I spend hours of thought untold
And not a single shout can span the spaces;

Wider those lakes may spread, and mountains heave,
Widening the world of snowflaked grass;
The woods may widen, and the winter leave
An emptier space where fewer grey wings pass;

And higher the clouds may roll, and empty grey
Streak with adumbraged black the boundless sky;
And wider may rivers slowly roll and stray
A-wandering on yielding land now dry;

But distance can never deter my internal devotion;
A tear is more real and more great than a somnolent ocean.

Winter #1

Why does the winter wind so fiercely blow
That bushes turn to sepulchres in the snow
When their branches, frozen and cold and firmly laden
With manacles of ice, can scarcely bend
Before they snap and are buried in snow and are hidden?

Formations—eddies and swirls in the uppermost air—
Penetrate down to us, layer by layer by layer;
Their courses are broadcast, dauntingly, forth
By scientists tracking whither they blow and they trend
And from whence they have blown, from their lair in the
    north;

Thousands there are of reasons for the forces
That push the northern winds along their courses;
Impossible to stop or to subdue,
With pity, none have anything to do.

Winter #2

Now Winter comes, bold and bare and bleak,
A riding man on a stark and naked steed,
Spying where Fall revenge had tried to wreak,
Setting aside each wounded branch to bleed,

Conquering, with invective, sunset's dark,
Riding astride his charger's naked back,
Charging ahead into his wintery work,
Breathing his frost upon the forest's black,

While the treetops sit, unquiet with late birds,
Etched with a filigree fret against the sun,
Whose elegance, when rising, writes, with words,
Sceneries of death against going down;

But goddesses wait, high-breasted like the Spring,
Ready to soar to waken Everything.

Winter #3

Although the thin grey-gold of winter's light
Drags in its footsteps, half forlorn, the glow
Of a veritable brightness, sheet of white
Across the frozen rifts of broken snow,

Glow is not what I seek; for I have tired
Of endless hope aborn of isolation,
Away from you but knowing I have fired
A spark in you from my new inspiration;

But I would rather more, a touch, a look
From your fine-fettered eyes of brown bedewed,
A smile, encouragement that this my book
Be more than languished longing, more imbued

With a spark of some completion, something done;
Then will a glow on snow desymbolise the sun.

Wit

Somehow the wit and laughter all have gone,
As if the sun forgot that he had shone
On sunny landscapes, decorated green,
With gala blue above an upturned scene,

And as I write of that enormous sky
That seemed to fill the days that passed us by,
It seems to melt and fuse to match your eyes
That endlessly regale me with surprise

That such emblazoned colour could exist
In a single glance no poet could resist.
But now the wit and laughter all have gone
And only pleasant memories live on

Captured, enraptured, in glorious array,
Radiant suns in a bitter winter's day.

Wonderings

Were all my wonderings to fade to mist,
And vanish like a smoke upheld by wind,
Still would your beauty glide, caparisoned
By winning reason no one could resist;

And were my heartfelt anticlines of praise
To tumble to a rock-strewn mound of schist,
Grey, littered over with clutter, stony grist
From my mental mill, still would your beauty raise

Monuments from that empty rubble pile;
And were my verse to cease to pour to glaze
The dawning steadfastness of future days,
And only calculations fill my file—

Still would my mind continue to compose
And paraphrase your smile in open prose.

Wood

And in the green and dawnlight of the wood,
I felt my heartbeat stagger as you smiled;
Your eyes entranced the trees and, like a flood,
The images of forests flooded wild;

All over in a breath, the sceptic sighs—
An ancient story savoured in a flash:
The flanked invasion of a mind by eyes
That mould its thoughts with whiplight like a lash;

Ah me, the old man sighs, oh for those days
When I too felt the golden gaze of youth
And reconnoitred round the looker's gaze
Looking in fervoured fever for the truth;

Ah me, oh my, how wise are those around
Who dare not tread upon forbidden ground.

Words #1

If you will only let me tune the words
As woods the spring-swept open eyries tune,
Then I am free to conjure into chords
A world quite free of slow-spun sun and moon;

But if you chide, resentful, spurning, churning,
How, in your heart, you'd feel too much restrained
Were you to be a patron of my yearning,
Then I would hide those verses, unattained;

So let me just out, once, from my self-made cage,
Cast off conquests torn from dragon's eyes,
Free, unconstrained in spread, let me assuage
The sorrows of my self-reproaching sighs

And integrate you into simple song;
And maybe I can right now what was wrong.

Words #2

"How weary, flat, unprofitable, stale"—
Thus in great heavy words the woeful heart.
"Flat" is the down-decry to colours pale
And "stale" the false flavour of unnatural art;

"Unprofitable" is the labour cold and dry,
Being dulled by non-achievement in the soul;
"Weary," the hand that lifts the pen awry
And tries to cast new carbon from old coal;

"Resonant" is the word Ambition calls;
"Resonant" is the outcry from the Muse;
"Resonant" echoes in the empty halls
That house the hapless whom the Graces lose;

But *what* is resonant? Only this sounds true:
My anger that this verse replaces you.

World #1

In this vast world of quiet and eased content,
There is a tone that strikes reverberations
Of elements not wholly innocent,
Casting, in smoothened seas, incarcerations

Of solemn passions lost; in murmured night,
Where cold stars shine with passionless intent,
There is a sound of muffled day and light
That breaks the peace with light incontinent;

Light is what breaks the murmured noise of peace;
Light takes on tone in synaesthetic voice,
And, with a gleam as beautiful as Greece,
Calls on the night to falter and rejoice;

For, though a heart can to one soul be pledged,
The knife of love is often double-edged.

World #2

Why, in this world that will not be all light,
Should not a moment's light gleam on forever
In lines that are not vague or recondite
But simply state the fact that we are clever

To build upon a tangled intercourse
Of glances, conversation, mutual looks,
A subtle overload of quiet force
That bonds us stronger than our work or books?

Yes, clever it is, and that is not too good
A word, for it has overtone of greed
And shallowness, a talent understood
As over-conscious, strained, a will unfreed;

But what we both desire is part fulfilled;
And inner pain within us both is stilled.

World #3

If I let you go, would my world be clear and I
Ungratefully retire from your affection,
Sunk in a world in which I dared not cry?
Or would I grieve at what would be defection?

If I let you go, would I then miss your smile,
The warm and perfect roundness of your arms?
Or would I find some way to reconcile
My loss by loving older women's charms?

If I let you go, could I forget your eyes
That burn these lines out from me, day by day,
And resurrect this endless enterprise
Each morning that I know you are away?

If I let you go, would I then feel less free?
Would *you* feel free if you let go of me?

X

X the third letter is of "zyxomma,"
A dragonfly that flits 'neath Indic skies
And skims across its waters hover-wise,
Like one I saw in Upper Canada;

The latter lent a scintillance to the sun
As each quick movement sped it, on its pond,
From plant to plant, then over and beyond
The furthest reeds, until reunion

With landfall's empty space revamped its course,
Swiveling it, in a moment miniscule,
To retro-trace its graceful path and fool
Its prey into thinking it had lost its force;

That slender slant of body formed of blue
Embodied East and West as one, not two.

Y

"Zyxomma," with its second letter Y,
Is a genus of Indian dragonfly
With narrow face and prominent eye
Of the family *Libellulidae*;

"What's in a name?" asks the balladeer
Who wants to pull his listeners near
And link their minds with the offspring dear
Created by Nature's biosphere;

A name is a sound that a human tongue
Can render to Heaven or address to dung;
A name is a necklace vowelly hung
With consonants on it, loosely strung;

A name is a label we use to allot
Lovers and dragonflies into a slot.

Z

It's Z that "zyxomma" starts, which is
The final word in the lexicon
Of all the better dictionaries,
Their last word we can brood upon;

Omm comes from the Greek for "eye";
And *zyx* from *zeuxis*, also Greek,
Meaning a "joining"; this dragonfly,
Possessing a head that is rather unique

In holding two eyes so closely conjoined
That they seem like one, would horrific be
To an animalcule that was not blind,
To a juvenile that could clearly see;

The zyxomma like a Gorgon seems,
Who threatens poets in their dreams.

.

CPSIA information can be obtained at www.ICGtesting.com
Printed in the USA
242557LV00001B/32/P